DATE DUE

APR 16 1985		
G OCT 2 1 1986		
G NOV 2 6 1986		
M APR 4 1987		

TEACHING

THE
MAGIC OF DANCE

Jacques d'Amboise

Hope Cooke

Carolyn George

SIMON AND SCHUSTER • NEW YORK

Photographs by Carolyn George

Copyright © 1983 by Jacques d'Amboise,
Hope Cooke and Carolyn George
All rights reserved
including the right of reproduction
in whole or in part in any form
Published by Simon and Schuster
A Division of Simon & Schuster, Inc.
Simon & Schuster Building
Rockefeller Center
1230 Avenue of the Americas
New York, New York 10020
SIMON AND SCHUSTER and colophon
are registered trademarks of Simon & Schuster, Inc.
Designed by Edith Fowler
Manufactured in the United States of America

10 9 8 7 6 5 4 3 2 1
Pbk. 10 9 8 7 6 5 4 3 2 1

Library of Congress Cataloging in Publication Data

d'Amboise, Jacques, 1934–
    Teaching the magic of dance.

    1. Dancing—Study and teaching—New York (N.Y.)
2. Dancing and children. I. Cooke, Hope, 1940–
II. George, Carolyn.   III. Title.
GV1788.5.D35 1983   793.3'07   83-11990
ISBN 0-671-46077-3
        0-671-49401-5 Pbk.

ACKNOWLEDGMENTS

Now I know what writers mean when they say "I owe it all to my editors." Alice Mayhew and Ann Godoff with imagination and abundant talent gave generously of their abilities to this project and made it happen. Edith Fowler, an artist and delightful person, from the very first meeting always brought, in addition to extraordinarily good taste, a little sunlight. They grace their profession and their publishing house.

JACQUES D'AMBOISE
New York City
April 1983

This book is dedicated to the teachers who taught me,
with a growing sense of appreciation
for the style and genius they brought to our profession.

INTRODUCTION

Jacques d'Amboise is a man with a vision, a man obsessed with the notion that dance should be an everyday part of people's lives—particularly young people. He is obsessed with the notion that exposure to the arts, and dance in particular, is healthy, creates discipline, literally transforms. He's seen it happen, his work over the last eight years with the National Dance Institute has proven it. This is a book about teaching; but teaching without books and blackboards, without lecterns or lesson plans, and most of all without pretensions. We're about to spend a year watching Jacques teach a thousand New York City school kids, a group of cops, and even the deaf the magic that is dance.

> "Sometimes I think he was once a kid like us."—An eleven-year-old student from P.S. 40 commenting on his teacher Jacques d'Amboise

Jacques grew up Joseph Jacques Ahearn in the tough section of Manhattan's Washington Heights, the youngest of four children. Young "Joey" belonged to street gangs. "It was just like *West Side Story*," he remarks. Jacques' mother was ambitious for her family (Washington Heights wouldn't hold them) and was determined that her children be conscious of the arts. She dragged them to the opera and the ballet and, along with his older siblings, Jacques started taking ballet lessons. Later on his mother talked George Balanchine, the great choreographer and artistic director of the New York City Ballet, into taking Jacques on as a student in exchange for which his older brother John would wash the studio floors. Jacques says, "It was kind of an old world exchange of favors, like bringing the local doctor a chicken." By fifteen he quit high school to join the New York City Ballet, starting

THREE PHOTOS: MARTHA SWOPE

12

a career that would raise him to superstar status in the ballet world, which continues to this day.

Jacques teaches by being Jacques—energetic, committed, always professional, unwaveringly honest. "The single most important thing in working with children," Jacques says, "is to communicate an honest love of what you're doing. They're all walking around with little lie detectors—one false note and you're out." His classes mirror the man and as such provide a good look at what makes for extraordinary teaching. Here is d'Amboise trained in Russian technique, infused with a European respect for inherited tradition, discipline, and good manners, who remains at heart a New York City street kid. And that's exactly how he teaches—he is a human link between St. Petersburg and Hell's Kitchen.

"He's sort of a cross between the Jolly Green Giant and Rocky."—Student, age twelve, from St. Patrick's School in New Jersey

The National Dance Institute started as a way for Jacques to introduce his own sons to dance without their "feeling forced to take lessons." Jacques approached his children's school and requested "a place, an hour, and if possible a piano." Then he told his sons to invite some of their friends to dance class. Six very hesitant little boys appeared for the first class clad, according to d'Amboise's instructions, in "whatever you would wear to play ball." And then they began . . . and with them so did NDI.

Jacques offered his program to other schools, phoning startled elementary school principals and saying, "Hi, I'm Jacques d'Amboise, the dancer. Would you be interested in having a dance program in your school?" He had only two requirements: first, boys only; and second, classes must be held during school hours. Boys only because Jacques was determined to knock down the sissified image of male dancers (although he allowed girls in later on). And by assigning time within the regular school day principals and teachers show the real importance they place on dance as an activity. "Besides," Jacques says, "after-school play shouldn't be structured by authority. That time is special for a child, it should be his own and it should be free."

Now, ten years after his first class, the National Dance Institute is a non-profit organization employing five full-time teachers and three musicians and reaching over a thousand fifth-, sixth-, and seventh-grade schoolchildren in almost every ethnic and socioeconomic category imaginable. Several of NDI's teachers are black males, reflecting Jacques' concern that the Institute should reach out to black boys in particular. There seems to be an unconscious desire in the programs offered by the Institute to break stereotypes and attack the notion that some kinds of people (boys, cops, the deaf) can't or shouldn't dance.

Jacques teaches a special evening class for the New York City police (last of the macho bastions). And his interest in teaching the hearing-impaired arose from his certainty that exposure to dance was one of the last things these children would be offered. All of Jacques' communication gifts are brought to bear on his work with the deaf, which relies heavily on his ability to relay intention through touch, expression and eye contact.

> "We can come here after arresting someone for grand larceny and just let all the tension out."—A veteran New York City policeman on the merits of dance class

Now that the National Dance Institute is established as a regional organization in the New York area, the Institute aims to expand its program throughout America. Jacques would like to establish local chapters of NDI with back-up teacher workshops in key cities across the country. The funding for the artist-in-residence programs would be picked up by the local school districts. Jacques' role would be to catalyze the communities' efforts to institute self-sustaining dance programs for their schools.

The NDI program is performance-oriented. The children are not just chosen for the program; they are selected through an audition process. Jacques feels strongly that the difference between dance and exercise is that dance, by its nature, demands a public expression. The children need a showcase to exhibit their excellence. All the exercises and routines Jacques and the other teachers give the children are leading up to something—a performance at year's end in Madison Square Garden. One thousand kids get together for the first time for this extravaganza—called the Event of the Year—that is the culmination of all their hard work. *Teaching the Magic of Dance* is a record of that year-long trip the children make from recruit to pro, from fifth grader to dancer.

SCENE ONE

He always takes the stairs, going up or down, because it's better for his knees. The metal staircases frighten him. But the children go up and down them at breakneck speed, seemingly without looking where they're going. Maybe it's just old age and aches and pains and accumulated injuries, but he goes *very* carefully and he holds on to the rail.

Those little eyes size you up immediately. They don't seem to be interested; you could be an obstacle and yet you know that they're curious and wondering, Who's he? Once I heard a kid run by me and yell out, "He's a plainclothes cop, a copper, undercover cop."

Some of them have seen me on TV, or they know I'm a dancer, maybe they've heard that I'm coming to their school. Sometimes as I walk by I can hear, "That's Chuck, Chuck Danboyce," or "Jock," or "Jock the dancer," or, "That's that famous French guy." Sometimes some children will stop after they pass me and turn around, fight their way back through the stream of children, come up to me and say, "Hey, haven't I seen you on TV?" or, "Aren't you somebody—a dancer?"

"You'll find out. You'll find out." I always try to present a little mystery whenever I can.

Two boys meet each other on the stairwell. One is white, with curly hair, skinny, skinny, skinny, with poppy blue eyes, and nervous, a high-pitched voice. He asks, "Where ya going, Brian?"

Brian is a squat, solid, round black boy. His laconic answer in a slow, deep, but sweet voice: "Dance class."

"Huh?" Josh, an athletic-looking white boy, says.

Brian repeats himself. "Dance class."

"What, you mean that ballet stuff?"

"I don't think it's ballet. It's kind of a jazz. Why don't you come?"

"No. That ballet stuff is for sissies." As Josh is running off, yelling "That ballet stuff is for sissies, it's for girls," Brian answers, but not very loud, as if he doesn't care whether Josh hears or not, "Nope, it's for boys," and goes on down the stairs. This whole conversation between Josh and Brian has been overheard by a perfect ghost.

He's very small with reddish hair and a wonderful texture to his skin, bluish, almost translucent. . . . His eyes are piercing, a reddish brown, almost a copper color, penny eyes. Andy the lurker, I later call him because he's always lurking on the outskirts of everything. Andy has overheard Brian and Josh's conversation while he was on his way up the stairs. Unnoticed, he backtracks and follows Brian down the stairs and into the lunchroom where the dance class is to be held.

The lighting is awful. Neon lights all over the ceiling. One entire bank of windows opens up to the street and throws in some sunlight. The room is two hundred feet long by a hundred feet wide, most of it taken up with lunchroom tables which have long benches attached to them. The floor is linoleum, a gray-green linoleum, and it seems as though the walls are the same color. At one end is the cafeteria and the kitchen with a serving area behind it where kids go with their trays to get their milk and sandwiches.

Jacques, and Michael, the pianist, with the five or six boys they've commandeered, are pushing the lunchroom tables with their benches, stacking and shoving them toward one end of the room to make a dance space. Michael is a thin nervous man in his late twenties. He is skinny and mustached, and is struggling hard to drag an upright piano to a position of more prominence so that he can see the dance space. Making the task more difficult is the fact that the piano only has three wheels. Holding up one end is a thin, blond woman in a running outfit, Miss Buckley, the gym teacher.

If there are five or six boys assisting Jacques and Michael, there must be another thirty or forty in the room running, sitting, laughing, rolling on the floor, giggling in the corners, taking full advantage of the fact that their gym teacher and the adults in the room are occupied, have their eyes off them.

As they push, Miss Buckley explains the constituency of the school to Jacques. "I wouldn't call this a neighborhood school—we've got maybe twenty children that are bused in from Harlem. We've got students from Queens, Brooklyn— Sheepshead Bay—that's because it's a working area. Because it's not a neighborhood school the parent body is not very active. A small nucleus, five or six women, do all the work. The PTA meetings are poorly attended. Probably three-quarters of the students are from single-parent homes. Single-parent fathers don't enter in much—except if a child has terrific problems, the father will be called in."

Once space has been made with all the lunch tables pushed back, leaving an area fifty by fifty feet, and the piano is set in position, Jacques asks Miss Buckley, "Is this everybody?"

Miss Buckley answers, "Yes, this is everybody in the first class."

"What do you mean, first class?"

She says, "Well, you are going to look at the other kids in the other classes."

"We only want to take around twenty kids!" he says. "There's already thirty-five, forty in the room!"

An embarrassed look comes on her face. "I know, but you've at least got to look at them. They all want to try out."

"How many more are there? We only have an hour. We have to be in another school."

"There are four other classes. And they all want to audition. And this is only the first class that's been told to come down."

"Four other classes! That's a hundred and twenty other kids! We're only having one class in this school!"

A look of terror crosses her face. How is she going to explain to those 120 other kids that he can't even look at them? When he sees her expression, he says, "Okay, we'll do the best we can."

He turns around, claps his hands and yells to the kids: "Everybody in the center! Hurry up! We don't have time! We've got lots to do! We've got lots to do!"

"He doesn't waste a second," Michael Rice says of Jacques. "I've never seen someone work like that before. The time element is probably the basis of his discipline, and I personally think that dancers are the most disciplined of all artists. The concentration necessary to dance develops your attention span."

Miss Buckley asks, "Shall I introduce you?"

"No. No, I don't need it, just let me go."

Every single time I've been introduced by either a teacher, the principal of the school, the superintendent, or anyone, there's a note of apology. It's as if they're saying, "This is a famous dancer, and he's come here to work with you and, kids, we gotta treat him right"—when all I want to do is make 'em dance, and they're gonna like it or not, and that's all there is to it.

I've got thirty kids sitting on the floor staring up at me. Within seconds, I can pick out the ones who are shy, the ones who are ringleaders, and spot the lurkers over in the corner.

I can spot them all within seconds. It's just like when I see a ballet dancer for the first time, I only need to look at one or two steps and I know what they're capable of.

I always introduce myself. "I'm Jacques d'Amboise, and I'm a dancer, but I'm also a teacher. And I'm a terrific dancer, but I'm an even better teacher. In fact, you're not going to find anyone who can teach what I teach better. I'm here in your school to teach, and you know what I'm teaching?"

They all stare at me. Of course they know, they're here

for a dance class, but they wait to hear it from me. "We're here to dance. And it's not ballet. Because ballet's too hard for you, and you're not good enough for ballet. It's gonna be jazz and you're gonna need sneakers!" The faces all look down at their sneakers as if they want to make sure they have them. "You need comfortable clothes. They don't have to be old clothes, but comfortable clothes, because you're gonna sweat, do rolls on the ground and knee slides—but mostly you're gonna jump."

I emphasize jumping because it's *magical*. It is leaving the earth. Fighting against being earthbound. You can capture the imagination of any child by saying, "He leaped in the air and it seemed like he was going in slow motion, and he looked around to see where he was going to land, and then he landed, and he made no noise when he landed, just like when a bird comes down." Jumping fills the imagination with the possibility of magical flight. You leave the ordinary and inhabit the air.

I've got them all psyched up with the idea of being in the air; then I turn around and I focus on a kid at random and say, "You! What's your name?" I don't just say "You" and wait. I say, "You, what's your name?" He's scared. He's either going to run, or he's going to fight. Now he's found out all he has to do is give his name. So he says, "Harry." And I say, "Okay, Harry." Now he's nervous, he thinks he's going to have to get up and dance. "Who's the best jumper in class besides you?" Relieved, he gets up, looks around at his friends. He starts looking around. "Pick somebody quick or I will," I say. Now he usually picks a friend. Or maybe an enemy, I don't know. But generally it's a friend.

Now that guy's on the spot. Now I say, "Okay, fella, come up here." He picks Joe, a skinny black kid who must be the best athlete in the class. Probably great at basketball. Joe gets up slowly and shuffles forward. I point to the floor and say, "You see that spot?"—usually a piece of tape, a mark on the floor—and I say, "Stand right on it. Now jump." And he jumps. "Now higher, come on." Now he jumps as high as he can.

I say, "Fine. Now bend your knees when you're up there. Good! Good!" And I say, "Pick somebody else." Then he picks one or two other guys and goes to sit down, and I say, "No, no, no, you only did three jumps, that was too easy. All three of you guys come up here. All right now, Joe, you jump in the air like you just did, and the others follow."

So now all three are jumping. "Now, Joe, when you're up there, make a whole turn, turn to your right, completely revolve in the air, and come back down on the same spot where you started." He looks at me thinking it's too hard. So I show 'em. I jump in the air, I revolve completely around,

and I land without any noise, and I freeze. And all the kids
stare with their mouths open. Now Joe gets ready; he's on
the spot. And he jumps, and he turns, and he lands, but he
staggers, and I say, "Ha! You moved! The jump was good, in
fact, I didn't expect you to do that well, but you moved at the
end. You gotta freeze. But you don't get another chance yet.
Your friends do, you picked them."

Now the two friends jump and one of them *does* it, but he doesn't quite get all the way around. And then the other one does it, but falls down, and everybody laughs. I say, "If you're down, stay down. Don't move." Now I turn back to Joe and say, "Okay, Joe, jump!" Now Joe does it, and he does it perfectly. And I say, "Terrific." I turn my back on him and I look at the other kids, and say, "The record is twenty-six times. In the other school a kid did this jump twenty-six times in a row, on a dime. And didn't stagger once. Go ahead, Joe."

Now it's a test. One jump, then two, two, then three, four . . . now, I do everything I can to help him. Sometimes I say, "Stop, Joe, you're up to six, take a big breath. Ready? Go, Joe. Stop. Good. Get your knees loose under you." Rarely does anybody ever do it. At this stage, if I didn't get everybody else up and dancing, I'd begin to lose them. Because now they've become spectators. So I say, "Everybody get up and try it." A mad rush. They all do it. Some fall, and some end up facing another direction, and quite often I'll stop them halfway through and I'll say, "Very good, except half of you turned to the left instead of to the right."

After a few tries, I make them all sit down. They've jumped, they've done something difficult, and they've participated in an athletic way. Now I tell them, "Very good. You did that great. But that stuff is easy. I'm going to give you something else that looks so easy you're going to say 'Ah, it's nothing.' But it's not. I need a volunteer." Now the hands start scooting up. Out of thirty boys, fifteen, twenty hands go up. I point to some kid who didn't raise his hand and say, "I'm glad you volunteered. Come on. You! Come up. I'm glad you've volunteered, what's your name?"

"Brian."

"Brian what?"

"Brian Drummond."

"Good, like Bulldog. Step on your right foot and take four steps forward and then four steps back." Most children —if not most, a good half—will step on their left foot instead of their right. The reason is, they're so anxious not to make a mistake, to step on their right foot, that they put all their weight on their right foot. They're thinking, My right foot, and they get ready, their weight's on their right foot, and then they go to step on it but they can't. So they step on their left.

Brian does the four steps forward perfectly. And then he does four steps backward, each time starting with the right foot. I'm amazed. It looks so simple and it sounds simple but it's not. I figure I'd better make it a little harder; I've got a real good one here. "Okay, take two steps front and two steps back." And that's quite hard. You need one or two steps to begin to pick up natural momentum. And then you ride that

momentum. You just begin to adjust your body to that momentum when you have to reverse it back. Just as you reverse back, you have to reverse front again. Two steps back, two steps front, two steps back. If it's four steps front, you have time to adjust, and it's much easier.

And again Brian does it perfectly. I say, "Wow! I'm surprised you did it that well. If he can do it, everybody can do it. Up, let's go." The whole purpose is to use people as examples, as leaders. Let them go through the test and the others all follow.

In the dance classes, although he is engagingly spontaneous and physically demonstrative with the kids, Jacques remains very much the classic dance master, the professional. Although he jumps around, he's strict. He's animated and full of life. He makes living and learning enjoyable, but he's a disciplinarian. The children respond very well. He can be stricter than regular teachers because he's not bound by the Board of Education.

"I would be outraged if some teacher called my kid a

dope," Miss Buckley says. "But here Jacques sets these rules and they work for him. I wouldn't approve of his method in a classroom, because it hurts too many people. But in this situation it works. The key is the children trust him because they sense that he likes them."

The audition has three parts. The first two are jumping and walking, controlled movement. But these are just physical tests. The third part requires imagination and fantasy. And this is the most fun. He makes them all line up behind him with their legs wide, and tells them that all the movements they're about to do should be in slow-motion balance, as if they're balancing on a slow trampoline. He gets them to start pushing out with their hands as if they're pushing aside obstacles, seaweed or drapery.

Michael supplies the appropriate musical background. If it's jumping, there are staccato chords. If it's walking, there's a rhythm like a jazz or boogie-woogie or disco beat. Here he starts to play underwater music like the kind you hear in the movies.

I tell the kids, "You're pushing through seaweed; you're in a suit that looks like a space suit, but it's made to be under water, a diver's suit; you're wearing a helmet, looking through glass." And then I yell: "Coming at you is a shark! Everybody follow me! Left elbow to your right knee!"

And I start a forward roll, a slow-motion forward roll. "Knees to the chest, slow motion, back to your hands and feet, turn around, wait! You just rolled right underneath that shark, he just went over your head. Yikes! A giant clam has got your foot! Quick, cover your ears, because look above! The lifeline's been cut! The dirty rat on top of the water cut the lifeline! Your enemy! Your ears are bursting! Water's filling your knees, water's up to your hips, water's up to your ears." I start holding my ears. "You're screaming! Uh-oh, no noise underwater, you don't hear, just open your mouth!" And I start fainting, and going down, and by now they're all involved, and everyone's lying flat on the floor, and I say, "Shh. Don't move. Everybody quiet." Michael cuts off the music. "Glub, glub, glub," I say. "That was the last of your air bubbles going up."

At this point Jacques gets up and says, "Listen, I've got a lot of other classes to look at. And I'd like to take everybody in this class. But I can't. So, we've got to quickly run through every step till we're done. First the jumps and turn to the

right. Next the four steps front, four steps back. And last of all, the underwater ballet that we invented. Quickly, let's go through with them. First the jump to the right."

Everybody jumps to the right, and he immediately says, "Okay, you, you, you, you, you, go over to the left. Stay over on that side." And he says, "Keep going, you're going to do the next step too, I just want to separate you so that we have two groups. You five guys I picked are the gold team."

He picked them because they jumped to the left, not the right. Not that they didn't jump high, but several times they've done it now; they have a right-left problem. Which means he may make a point of taking them in the class, because they need the help. Or, if he sees they don't try then they're the ones for sure to be dropped.

I call them the gold team so that they think they're special. Next I spot their walking forward, four steps front, four steps back, two, two, two—which is not just dexterity, it's rhythm; they've got to stay on the beat. Every once in a while I'll yell, "Freeze!" And they have to stop, and if they're not in the correct position with the right leg front, or the left leg front, whichever the correct leg is, I say "Ah, you've got the left leg front, good for you; but it should be the right—go join the gold team."

When you do something like that you can see doubt and confusion on the faces of the kids who have the correct leg front, but never Brian Drummond. He'll stop and think Why, and then he'll not have an answer. You'll almost see him think, I'll find out later—there must be a reason; I've done what I was ordered, I did it correctly.

When we do the underwater thing, I size up those that really do it with enthusiasm and effort, those that are kind of half embarrassed and giggling about it, and those that keep nudging their friends and laughing. I watch and wait till it's over and say, "Okay you, you, you, you, come on, join the gold team." Now we have two teams.

I ask Miss Buckley to get the names of these boys, and I go over to talk to the gold team. "Listen here, we only have so much room. And what I want to do is make a whole team like you, and the next class is going to have their gold team. And at the end of the day we'll see how many are in the gold team and how many in the regular class. And if we can have an extra class at this school, it'll be the gold team's class."

The kids are kind of numb because I use the term gold team, indicating something special. So they're all psyched up to think that they're the ones that made it. Except some of them are smart enough to know that they didn't make it 'cause they didn't try, and then there are some that didn't try because they didn't really want to be in it, and they are a little nervous that somehow they made it. They don't understand. So when it seeps through that what has happened is the regular class is going to be the dance class, and that they're on a waiting list, there's some disappointment. And perhaps there's some secret relief that they're not going to have to commit themselves. It's all very much involved with

the personality of the child; some don't want to take a chance.

As I walk over to Miss Buckley I can hear the conversations coming from the gold team. There always seems to be one kid who's been punching another kid and giggling and laughing throughout class, who announces, "Well, I never wanted to make this class anyway. All this dancing stuff is for sissies."

One child who hasn't been participating but kind of lurking in the corner is Andy, the frail little boy with reddish hair. I hardly notice him, except for the fact that when I say, "Okay, everybody up now to dance," everybody gets up and tries, except this one little boy. I would never have noticed him except that everybody's dancing except him.

"Hey," I call to him, "Are you going to be part of this class?"

And it's almost as if he shrinks a little bit, and gets even smaller, and he seems imperceptibly to move back six inches or so, yet his feet . . . and his little head kind of shakes No, and his tiny little rosebud lips open up and whisper, "Just watching."

SCENE TWO

Back to the same lunchroom a week later. This time it's filled with the sixty children Jacques has chosen for the regular class. There's another sixty or so, the gold team, waiting for openings. Nina, part of the NDI staff and a talented dancer in her own right, is putting the kids through a very vigorous warm-up exercise that is a mixture of dance steps and calisthenics. She is a very attractive woman, blue-eyed, with beautiful bone structure, of medium height, with a strong, sturdy dancer's body. Nina will work with Jacques and, more often than not, start the class as he dashes from one school to another.

Jacques bursts in, making a point of not interrupting the exercise. He walks around the periphery, keeping his back to the children, not looking at them. They'll take any opportunity to stop the exercises to yell, "Hey, Jacques, there's Jacques."

I want them to learn that when dancing all their attention should be focused on their exercise, on their teacher. Sometimes when they see me come in they stop the exercise. If that happens I feign anger and say, "No stopping! Keep exercising," and then I leap in and join them. I get right behind Nina and say, "What's next, Nina?" and I look at her and pay strict attention to her. There can only be one leader and at this point, Nina is conducting this class.

"It's cadence," Nina says. "Jacques pushes the kids to their limits until it looks like they're going to break and then he comes back and picks them up. A little dangerous, but he

doesn't give them anything they can't handle. The key to good teaching is the ability to keep the child on the edge of his seat. Sometimes it might seem too fast-paced or driven. But it's good to be a step ahead. Jacques works with a slam-bang let's-get-involved-and-feel-it energy. He doesn't ask them to feel the various elements of dance as teachers from a modern dance background tend to. He says just, 'Do it,' and then you see what happens. When the child gets it without thinking about each step you'll know he's got it. He puts the kids on the line. Makes them be their best. What they're getting is a taste of being a performer.''

When Nina finishes the exercises, she says, "How do you want to run the class today, Jacques?"

And he says, "No, you run it, you tell me. What have you been doing? Do you have something to show me?"

"We've only done the warm-up exercises," she says, "but we have one step that I was working on."

He says, "Great! Show me."

Jacques feels something touching his arm and he turns around and finds it's Andy.

"Can I talk to you?" he asks.

"Not now! Not now! Nina's going to show us a step! Here," he says, not wanting to hurt Andy's feelings, "here, sit down, let's watch."

I put my arm around Andy and we sit down together and I forget about him as I involve myself in watching what Nina's working on. She's doing some floor move which is the kind of stuff I wouldn't ordinarily give them.

One of the strengths of the National Dance Institute is that we have a lot of teachers with diverse abilities and styles. My style is energetic, with a lot of vigorous foot movements, and it predominates, but each individual teacher brings his own technique to bear and the students profit from the exposure.

Little Andy is tugging at my sleeve again. "I want to be in the dance class." I ignore it. I'm not even sure what he said. I'm busy watching Nina.

"I'm a good dancer."

And I say, "What?"

And his little face looks up, with those little penny eyes and he says, "I'll try very hard."

"What are you talking about?"

"I want to be in the dance class," he says.

"But we can't take any more; you should have been here for the audition." And he says, "I was."

"Well, what happened? Maybe you're on the gold team?"

"No."

"Oh. Well, then you should be in here. We only have the gold team and the regular team. You should be in it." He gets up and runs to join the other children.

Miss Buckley comes over to me and asks, "Are you adding more? I'm so glad you took Andy."

"What do you mean? I didn't take him, isn't he in the class?"

"No. He didn't audition last week. But Andy really should be in, he's the kind of kid you want. He's great, he tries hard but he never seems to make it. He lacks the self-confidence and rarely takes a chance, but he seems to want to do this. His mind is full of fantasy, and it'll be awful if you don't take him."

"Okay. We'll take him, we'll see how he does, but he's gonna have to keep up."

Andy is a disaster. He keeps making mistakes. Getting under people's feet. If they go to the right he goes to the left. His legs and arms don't seem to follow the orders of his brain. Andy's brain sees everybody stepping on the right foot, and it sends the order late; by now everybody's switched feet and they're doing something else. He steps on his right foot but his left foot goes out. Then he tries to adjust, switch back to his right, and trips over his left foot as it's moving. It's a comedy, you couldn't invent such funny movement.

Nina looks aghast at this new addition to the class. When class is over, she comes over to me and says, "How did that kid get in?"

I say, "Oh! Well, ah, I put him in, it was a last-minute addition."

"But he's terrible!"

"Yeah, he is terrible, but look how hard he tries. We gotta keep him."

At the end of the second audition Jacques makes his selections for the "SWAT Team." The Swat Team is the Saturday class Jacques teaches at Lincoln Center for his most exceptional students, those for whom the regular classes are much too easy. "We can't take more than a few kids from each class; otherwise we'll have too many. Don't forget, we're teaching over a thousand children, and twenty schools, and if we take just a few from each, we'll already have sixty or a hundred."

Jacques says, "Nina, I need that kid Brian Drummond, he's absolutely fabulous. He's got to be part of the Swat Team. It's up to him of course, but tell him that he's invited to come. And this guy over here and that girl over there. That's all I want from here, unless somebody develops later on to be exceptional, then you can send them along."

When class is over, Nina calls the three of them over. Everyone is gone but Nina, Michael, and Jacques and the three children. Jacques says, "Listen. I've been watching you and you three kept a step ahead of everybody else. Faster than everybody else. Now, you know you're the best in the class, don't you?" They look at each other, swelling inside with pride. But trying to play it cool.

"Well, this class is going to be very boring. You're going to probably drop out because it's so uninteresting because we've got to spend time and make all those guys as good as you. And that's going to take a lot of time. You're going to be hanging around waiting for them to catch the steps that you get right away. So I have a proposition to make. I'm going to start a special class on Saturday morning, did you hear me? Saturday morning. It means if you want to do it you'll have

48

to give up a lot of stuff that you usually do Saturday morning. It's going to be at the New York State Theater . . . at Lincoln Center, and I'm not going to tell you how to get there, you're going to have to find out. Lincoln Center, New York State Theater, fifth floor. You gotta be there Saturday morning at 9:30. And you're not going to be the best in class anymore, because there's going to be other kids from other schools that are as good or better than you and you'll be lucky if you can keep up. And I'm not going to stop to help anybody. I'm just going to throw hard steps at you. So, it's up to you. You show up if you want."

Miss Buckley says, "Jacques' fondness for people and his ability to make you believe he cares, his talent for finding and affirming the individual pulse of a person plus his projection of self-approval and self-confidence that makes you value his approbation is at the heart of his success. What's special about this program is not so much the dance but his passion to share it."

"Dancing," Jacques says, "performing together, has elements of religion—all together we make something larger than any individual. If it works everyone is touched by an indefinable essence of what it is to be more than human. You and the kids begin to work together. If they stick it out, both the teacher and the pupil are overwhelmed by the discipline they've been through together. It becomes a fantastic ritual experience that's so much bigger than anything they imagined when they came to take a dance class in a lunchroom!"

SCENE THREE

There's a doorman at the New York State Theater. Martin has gray hair and a pale face, a bit dour-looking. When I come in on Saturday morning around 8:30, Martin asks, "You're gonna have all those kids here today?"

He sounds gruff but I know him, and he's sweet. I say, "Yep! Sorry to bother you, Martin, but there'll probably be sixty of them, at least."

"What room you gonna be in?"

"The main hall, fifth floor, the big one. It'll be 9:30 to 10:30, but they'll be coming early and we might run over a little bit."

As I'm getting in the elevator, Martin calls out, "Tell all your kids not to play with the elevator buttons!"

I remind myself, I've gotta make an announcement in class, even though it won't make any difference; they're gonna play with the elevator buttons. I played with them, everybody plays with the elevator buttons! But I'll try.

Kids from eight to thirteen come to these Saturday morning Swat classes to rehearse for the Event of the Year, which is Jacques' Felt Forum dance extravaganza in May. Clumps of parents and younger siblings (reminiscent of Jacques' early introduction to dance when he tagged along to his older sister's rehearsals) ring the practice room, standing or sitting among multicolored piles of down jackets.

The walls are cinder blocks painted yellow; the floor is gray linoleum. The room is exactly the size of the New York State Theater stage underneath, sixty by eighty feet. Mirrors cover one wall, bars line all four walls—exercise bars—and fifteen or twenty fold-up chairs are scattered around the room. A black grand piano is over in the corner; the ceilings are lined with neon lights and some big scoop lights that can be focused. Jacques goes to the wall where all the light

switches are and pushes every switch. As early as he is, there are kids already there; there are always kids there ahead. They're playing at the piano, or just sitting around; they have sleepy eyes but they're all excited.

Jacques is wearing sneakers worn down at the sides. His feet are crippled from years of dancing. After many breaks and dislocations the second and third toes on each of his feet have been shortened, then webbed together to prevent further injury.

"I just can't stop moving," he says. "If I do it hurts too much." At dawn he runs around the Central Park reservoir and throughout the day he keeps active, exercising for several hours, dancing with his students, and in the ballet season rehearsing for performance. At forty-nine Jacques d'Amboise is one of the oldest dancers in the ballet world. Despite a certain ruefulness about his disability and the fact that he now often acts his way through the few performances he still gives, Jacques is not ashamed of being past his dancing peak. He has had it all and he is radiantly positive about the transformation of his career from dancer to teacher. Because a dancer's life is brief, he's learned to use every moment.

On this first day of the Swat Team, Brian Drummond is sitting at the piano and a couple of boys are sitting on the floor playing cards. There are two girls in the middle of the room practicing the warm-up exercises that Nina has given them. One of them has a heavy face, dark little black eyes—extraordinarily bright like little black holes—black eyebrows, black hair in two pigtails, and a short, stocky body. She's not obviously attractive, but she ends up being *beautiful* because of the intelligence and inquisitiveness, the openness of her face. Her name is Scarlett. With her is Lisa, pretty, blond, in Gucci pants.

I am amazed at how well they are doing the exercises. And the minute they see me, the gestures get stronger, the knee-bends deeper, and they count louder, they're showing off. I think, Good. They're performers. When they see me they don't do less and hide, they do more and blaze.

"Hiya, Brian," I yell over to Brian Drummond, who's sitting at the piano. "Hello, fellas," I say to the two playing cards. All early. Good. "What are your names?" I ask the two girls who are warming up. The first to speak up—in everything she's the first—is Scarlett. Big smile, but her eyes don't smile, her eyes devour me with curiosity, analyzing my reactions. She says, "Scarlett." And I say, "Like fire?"

"No, like O'Hara."

"Okay, Scarlett. What's your name?" I ask the other girl.

"Lisa," she says.

"Good, that's simple. Scarlett and Lisa."

"No! Fire!" Scarlett says, and I laugh, thinking I better watch this one. So I say, "Enough talking. Come on, since you're all early, let's start dancing and use the time." So the two boys put down their cards, and Brian leaves the piano and all of them start warm-up exercises, and within seconds some more kids come over; they were out in the hall, out in the john; they heard the piano stop—a lot more came earlier than I knew.

They were exploring the theater, looking at the costumes. They hear me yelling, hear my voice giving out the exercises, so they start coming out. As each of them comes out, I yell a greeting and keep dancing. I say, "Come on, join us, hurry up!" And they come and join us, and before you know it, fifteen kids are dancing away. From then on, we're launched.

Between then and 9:30, when the class officially starts, people will come in and join. Parents will come and sit. Or leave to go have breakfast. The room will fill up. By 9:30, most of the kids are there. And we will have already created some kind of a dance. I have no idea in advance what I am going to do. I make it up as I go along, and I tell that to the kids.

"I have no idea what we're going to do, but we're going to do something." I begin by throwing myself a challenge. "We're going to do something hard, and it's going to be a jump, and we're going to start by moving backwards." Now, I have to fulfill that framework. Then I'll add to it, I'll watch

and analyze. I'll divide the group, see which children respond, and I'm watching all the time to see who's slow. But generally speaking, I don't worry about it, because there isn't going to be any help, really, for the children in this class. If they can't keep up they'll quit on their own, because everyone's got to go ahead; or else they'll be ignored in the background—and when it comes time to perform the dance they won't be able to do it. And I tell them that, right at the beginning. No one's going to stop to help you. Unless you have a friend who'll take you in the corner. You keep up, or you get out of the class. The reason for this Swat class is exactly that, to keep momentum up. In their regular school, they were too good and they lost interest because the other people were too slow. So they come here, where we don't want anybody slow.

"You're the best dancers around. You've made the effort and have given up your Saturday mornings to come here. And I will give you steps that professional dancers would have trouble doing. But I'm not going to pay you a salary like the professional dancers because you're only dancing a couple of hours. They have to dance all day long and deliver the goods at night. Every day of the week. We just dance for a few hours once a week and at the end of the year do one performance. But I expect the same of you. If I had a thousand dollars, I'd pay it to you. But I don't. Professional dancers get paid, but not just for dancing. They have special things which you're going to have to have. They've gotta have strength and flexibility. They've got to have speed and a sense of time and energy. They've got to develop humility and modesty in the beginning. And then confidence and pride at the end. And too much of one or the other of these things gets in the way of reaching your potential. It must be the right chemistry and either you have it, or if you don't have it you're going to develop it here. And it will be wonderful. Because it's going to allow you to dance fantastically.

"When I was your age—eight, nine, ten—where I lived there was nothing but gangs on my block. If you went to one side of St. Nicholas Avenue, you were with all the blacks and you were fighting gangs so you would never go there, you would never go through their block or they'd get you. And you'd never see a black walk through our block, because we would get them. We'd say, 'If those blacks come to our block, we're going to get them.' No one ever knew what 'get them'

meant. Or what we would do. On the other side, the Broadway side, most of the older Jewish people lived, and it was a little bit more middle-class. We were poor. We would go raiding, breaking windows and stealing and breaking into cars.

"When you were eight years old you joined the Guerrillas; by the time you were thirteen or fourteen you were in the Panthers; fifteen, sixteen, seventeen you got into the Victory boys or the Fanwoods or the Vampires. At first it was nothing but playing sports and a little mischief and running errands for the big guys. But when you became a Panther, you graduated to petty crime. I had a friend in the Panthers who had his hand blown off with a homemade zip gun. Out of all the kids on my block, half became crooks. Some became policemen and some went into the church—priest, brother, nun. Some run porno shops on 42nd Street. I would have been one of those guys, except I'd slip out of the gang, take the subway downtown to my dance lessons. And at eleven years old I was performing, at fifteen I was earning a salary

and traveling through Europe on my own, and by seventeen I was making movies, I was a star. Why did this happen to me? Because very early on I got involved in something that was good, creative, magical, and something that captured me. Dancing saved me.

"And dancing had to do with me alone. I didn't need any gang to back me up, or to support me. It was you alone on the stage and you had to deliver the goods. And there's nothing like it. You face yourself and you have to discover yourself."

If I see anybody or anything in the room that captures me, I use it. Some parents may be sitting on the side and their children will keep looking over at them. I bring those kids right in front of their parents, and make the whole Swat Team turn and face the parents. Then I mime: I'm a ticket taker, and then I'm the usher, and then I announce, "Okay, now we're ready, we're going to perform, are you ready? Dance!"

And I make them do the dance we've just been working on for their parents. When they've finished I say loudly, "I want my money back. You're not ready to perform yet." Then I turn them around, tell them to face the mirror again, and say, "So stop performing for your parents until you're ready to perform for them. Then, knock them out! You'll be so good." That distracts them from the fact that there are people watching the class and feeling that they should be performing for them. They should learn to perform for a mirror or a wall. Or nothing. Or an audience. It's a skill that comes from imagination and training.

Every time I'm in a ballet class and feel that I need an extra push, I imagine that the entire Bolshoi Ballet, just arrived from Russia, is sitting along one whole side of the room, talking to each other in Russian out of the side of their mouths, saying, "These Americans, they're not very good." And as I walk forward to take my class, I think to myself, All right, you Russians, I'm going to show you great American dancing. I'm going to make you stop whispering.

By doing this I am practicing the skill of performing my best. When you go out on the stage, you don't see the audience, it's all black. All you do is follow spots; you're like a little bug under a microscope with bright lights on you. You have to reach those three thousand people out there in the dark and you've got to capture them so that they don't look at anybody else but you, and it's your job to see that they're delighted by what you do. It's a skill to develop. A skill of physical movement ordered by imagination.

The front line of children seems to be the most practiced or talented. Several of the little girls have their hair back in professional-looking ponytails and sport dancers' leg-warmers. The majority of the children are dressed in jeans, T-shirts, and every color and stripe of sneakers.

Nina helps Jacques teach the class; they dance together. "Nina, lead the girls in that step; boys, over here. Nina, lead the boys; I'll lead the girls. Girls, join the boys. You five boys over here."

He keeps switching the patterns and groups. He sets up competition and he breaks that competition, so that groups don't solidify. He never stays with large groups long, but goes back to working with individuals, never staying with them long either, always moving back to the group. No one ever stands or sits for more than a few minutes without having to get up and dance. Any time anybody does anything, it has to be done up to performance level and the others sit and watch intently because they have to get up and do it next. He asks for volunteers, and he appoints volunteers. He points to kids who haven't volunteered and makes them dance, swearing that they volunteered. No one is allowed not to dance.

I think the children learn when I make up ideas and steps directly in front of them, at the spur of the moment. I don't go in with any preconceived notions. I purposely don't try to flesh out the whole outline beforehand. The value of this approach is that the children see the honesty and openness of creativity in public. I goof, I make mistakes, I change things when I realize that what I did was not so good. And it is all right there in front of them. I'll say, "Try this step . . . I

have a wonderful idea, let's do it . . . come on . . . no, you didn't do it right . . . try again. . . ." After a while I'll say "Stop—we are not going to do that, it is a lousy idea, it doesn't work." And then I will try to explain why it doesn't work—it's too busy or there are too many steps. "I gave you too many things to do. We have to make it easier." What I'm doing is discovering in public the success or failure of my own creative process and the children participate. It's a very improvisational thing. There is an openness to the creative process. Choreographers are all afraid to admit they are wrong, they want to look sure—absolutely sure.

I think that openness is one thing that children gain from. I'm not afraid to say something right in the open, try it out and if it doesn't work to change it. The kids say, "He is hard and demands the most, but then he admits he is wrong when he makes a mistake." I learn all the time, I learn and relearn again.

In the midst of all that's going on I keep finding one kid underfoot. Always putting the wrong leg forward. And then it hits me. I finally realize this kid is Andy!

"Do the set from the beginning, everybody; Nina,

c'mere a minute. Nina, how did he get in the class? That kid Andy. What's he doing in here? He's terrible."

"Yeah, he's terrible, but look how hard he tries. We gotta keep him. Seems like I heard that somewhere," Nina says, grinning.

"But this is the Swat Team. It's supposed to be for the best of the kids. He's *never* gonna keep up! He'll *always* be a mess. What are you doing, letting him come in here? He's a disaster, just a disaster!"

"Jacques tries to reach as many children as possible," one of the parents says. "But when he sees that some have a special talent, he'll put them in a special program. He feels that they are slowed down by the others. It's cheating them as it's cheating the others *not* to challenge them. It's cheating them because they can go further, and faster. The way he has developed his program, he. can combine the two—people who are above average in talent and those who are merely motivated. This combination is what inspires." Maybe there's hope for Andy.

Jacques announces sometime during the first day of the Swat class that in addition to learning dance steps, the language of dance, they can learn the language of silent people, signing.

"There are a number of people around you—fantastic dancers—who, when you call their name or you say, 'Hey, you,' may pay no attention to you. It's because they don't hear you. If you see somebody lean over and hit another guy, what he's really saying is, 'Hey, you!' to his friend, who's deaf too. Watch how they talk with their hands and their expressions. I have them in this class because they're very good. And I think we should take the opportunity of learning their language. So, when you're dancing next to someone who's a signer, try and find out how you can say your own name, and how to say hello and goodbye in their language."

Jacques turns to the deaf children and says, "I'm glad to welcome you. One and two and three and four," he counts. "I" (points at self), "glad" (rubs chest in circular motion, palm flat), "meet" (brings two index fingers together, one from right next to the nose, keeping his hands in fists), "you," he exclaims (points toward the children as he stands on one leg, the other one lifted behind him, and pivots a full circle, tracing his finger across the whole audience and winding up with a quirky angulated bow).

"Now as for me, my name is Jacques." Jacques demonstrates, "It's a J." He sketches the letter J and then swishes his index fingers like kicking legs. "You see it's not J-A-C-Q-U-E-S spelled out, but J, and then Dancer, because that's what I do. Now I have to find out what your names are." And each of the children in turn signs his name.

"Teaching the deaf to dance has special rewards and special problems," Nina says. "Dance is not an odd thing for these children to be doing. Communicating, reading, language—these are hard tasks. Non-language activity that can be demonstrated nonverbally is a joy. It's nice to have a translator there but it's not essential. The children can do it anyway since it is nonverbal, and particularly with Jacques, as he is so emotive. He is a nonverbal communicator. There is a lot of hugging, a lot of body language, a lot of faces. He is very very natural with children. He never treats the deaf children as if they are different from the other children. He has to make some modification to communicate but he holds them to the same expectations that he has for the hearing. Their regular teachers, even their parents, don't expect so much. For some of the parents it's a revelation."

"There are dance therapists who say dance free, dance sad, dance joyous. Be a fish. Be a tree. It's not enough," Jacques says. "You need the self-discipline along with self-expression. The therapeutic aspect of dance will be a natural corollary if you're able to do something that's very difficult and you're able to master it through a lot of persistence. You don't have to dance the happy tree for it to be good for you or to feel good."

Near the end, before he has the warm-downs which finish each class, Jacques turns out the lights to test the ensemble's aplomb. The class ends in darkness with the thunderous stomping of sneakers amid the clatter of cymbals.

"FAT CITY"

Jacques, looking radiantly happy in paint-daubed jeans, begins the class with the warm-ups. He offers a warm smile to each newcomer who enters the New York State Theater rehearsal room.

Today he's casting for "Fat City," the dance the Swat Team and the police officers will be doing as the big act of the Felt Forum show. Although Jacques has referred to "Fat City" and has sung snatches of the lyrics— "Give back the fat, he needs his fat"—and talked about a gangster ballet, no one has any idea what the story will be.

"Now, we're going to learn some very hard dances," he tells the assembled members of the Swat Team. "We're going to make them up together, and perform them at the end of the year. Each of your schools is going to have a dance to do as well. But the Swat Team's routine will be the hardest. The dance is a story. I'm not sure what we're going to do, you have to be patient with me; but each Saturday as we go along, it will evolve. First of all, there's got to be a group of gangsters, tough mean gangsters, and their boss is gonna be a skinny nervous guy, real sharp and cool, black greasy hair, dark glasses, all dressed up in a zoot suit that's skin tight like a shark or a snake, and his name's gotta be something like, I don't know, Mugsy, or . . . let's call him Legs, Legs Diamond. 'Cause he always has diamonds, he loves diamonds. He sends diamonds to his girlfriend, he has diamond calling cards, and when he bumps you off, he leaves a little diamond in your lips. He's surrounded by gangsters, who are his bodyguards, his trusties."

All the boys try out for the gangster parts. Jacques runs through the steps, and those that catch on quickest he grabs and brings over to one side; there are about twelve of them in all; the most agile, the quickest learners, become the gangsters. After they're chosen, a funny thing happens. Jacques tells them, "You're gonna be dressed all in black, with shiny

white leather ties, and dark glasses, and a carnation in your lapel." As Jacques describes the costumes, the kids are transformed. In their mind's eye they're wearing dark glasses and moving in a slinky rough-tough gangsterlike way. They're already imagining . . . so they're already better, more creative, more like dancers.

"Okay, gangsters, sit down. On another day we'll work longer on this. But now, what we need is a victim. Let's make the victim somebody kind of big and establishment. Some big capitalist money man who runs the whole world, who has bankers and lawyers and real estate interests and he's surrounded by worshippers. Let's call him Mr. Fat. Mr. Fats, that's better.

"Whoever plays Mr. Fats doesn't have to be fat. We'll just wrap him up in foam rubber till he's round like a ball. A big fat roll of foam rubber. Mr. Fats has a big cigar, and he's

carried everywhere he goes. We'll get a whole bunch of strong dancers to carry him around." Jacques looks around for candidates and picks Castellucci, the skinniest, scrawniest little guy in class. He'll look like a little round ball, all wrapped up in foam rubber with his little head and his glasses, smoking a cigar; he'll look very funny. Castellucci looks at Jacques, a little unhappy, because in his imagination he'd envisioned himself as king of the gangsters, Legs Diamond. He doesn't realize that Mr. Fats is a fun role, a starring role.

"Okay, now we need some good guys who are going to capture these gangsters when they do something bad, so let's have cops. I need some cops." A whole bunch of boys want to be cops so Jacques says, "Now wait a minute. There are women cops too. And undercover cops. In fact, I teach cops." Everybody stares at him and their mouths drop open. "That's right. Every Monday evening right here, I teach undercover cops, officers on the narcotics squad, detectives. Sometimes they've just arrested somebody, or put someone in jail, or delivered a baby, or been to court, or found a lost child, or spent the day directing tourists how to find Radio City Music Hall or the Empire State building. Then at the end of the day, after doing all this kind of stuff, they come here and take a dance class. So we'll use them as cops in 'Fat City,' but they're not enough, they're big, but there's not enough of them. So we need a whole bunch of little cops."

Jacques picks most of the remaining boys to be cops, which makes them all excited. They love the idea. He adds a couple of deaf children in among the cops, and asks Sam Edwards, who's the deaf interpreter and signer, to help him. "Tell Curtis that he's a sergeant, but an undercover sergeant; he's got a gold badge, and it's inside his lapel. Underneath, so people don't see. And he carries a pistol on his ankle. He's very, very fast. He doesn't need a squad car, he can run down a crook on the street." Then Sam tells Curtis all that, and you can almost see the pride grow in him. Curtis is going to imagine that gold badge under his lapel, and he's going to imagine he can run fast, he's going to dance fast and try hard.

Jacques talks directly to the deaf kids, trusting Sam Edwards to translate. The children are clearly pleased by Jacques' individual attention. Jacques and Sam have a palpable bond of respect for each other's abilities as dancers and as men. Sam is in awe of Jacques' talent for communicating spontaneously with his whole being, something so important when teaching the deaf.

Sam is a hearing-impaired actor and dancer. He's a personality and a character and a courageous, wonderful soul. Skinny, ascetic-looking, he wears a strange little yarmulke-style cap in assorted blazing colors. He has an extraordinary sense of rhythm and timing, and a love of theater.

Sam just showed up once at the class I was teaching, fearlessly introduced himself with sign and a piece of paper and a pen. He reads my lips, and even more, he seems to read my mind. He wants to dance, wants to perform. I choreographed a dance for him and a deaf girl, a short little dance, and it was videotaped. Then I started working with the deaf children, and who showed up from out of nowhere but Sam! He just wanted to be around to help. I don't have any money to pay him, but he should be paid, he's wonderful. Little by little he took the deaf kids under his wing. He became a kind of mother hen, clucking around with his skinny arms outstretched, with all these little deaf kids around him. When they didn't feel like dancing because they were tired or lazy or unsure, he'd spot them. When they were unclear about which leg to be on, he'd watch them and help them. He learned faster than anybody. And danced everything beautifully. He was there all the time, ready to help. I have such confidence in him that, as with all great people, it's best to leave him alone. Their hearts are in the right place, their talents and minds are more than equal to the task; just leave them alone and they can't help but succeed. With Sam, you can't do any better. He doesn't need direction or help from me. I need to follow him.

"Now we've got the good guys who are going to capture the bad guys." Jacques reviews the plot. "And we've got Mr. Fats, who's going to get robbed of his fat. What we need is something that Mr. Fats did that was bad. Mr. Fats's gonna take over all of Times Square, tear down all the theaters and build something else, but what he doesn't know is that living in the basement of one of the theaters that he's gonna tear down is a whole family of orphan girls. This beautiful, eight-foot-tall gorgeous lady—like Wonder Woman—takes care of them, like a mother. I'll find some wonderful ballerina to be that mother, but we need orphans!"

All the little girls want to be orphans. The orphans are going to have to dance with the gangsters and the cops; we've got twelve gangsters, so we'll need twelve little orphans and twelve little cops. As Jacques picks the orphans, he points to one and says, "You—you are the saddest of all the orphans, 'cause something awful happened to you, but no one can get you to talk about it. And you know why they can't get you to talk about it? Because you have your thumb in your mouth all the time." Then he gives a few of the other girls something else to work with.

"You are not really an orphan," he tells one. "Because you have parents. But you ran away from home because they were mean to you. But what you don't know is that they really care about you, they're broken-hearted, and they're searching the city for you." Jacques tries to create a dramatic background for each child. It doesn't even have to show up in the dancing, but it becomes grounded in their imagination.

I start by making up sad poses, and I make them say "Woe" and "Oy-yoy-yoy" and "Mercy" and "Mea culpa" and "Help" and I ask them to think and say things like "poor" and "sad" and "dreadful," which they say out loud with every step that they take and each gesture that they make. They tear their hair, and they beat their breasts and they sob, and I invent some choreography to reflect those emotions.

"The Wonder Woman—let's make up a name, say Kitty —had an old boyfriend when she was in school, who was crazy about her. But she kind of forgot about him; she didn't even like him. His name was Harvey Shapiro. Harvey Shapiro had horn-rimmed glasses, pimples, braces on his teeth, and a squeaky voice; he was the laughingstock of the school. But he loved Kitty, who was a very sweet young girl (she wasn't as tall as she is now). But she never paid attention to him; she felt sorry for him; once she let him kiss her in the hall. They grew up and she went on to college, and married several times, divorced, had a farm, then she decided she didn't like any of that, what she was going to do was take care of orphans. Now guess what happened to Harvey Shapiro. He changed his name and started a new career. He's now known as Legs Diamond. The glasses are gone; he's got contact lenses. Those braces fixed his teeth. He's got diamonds on his fingers instead of pimples on his face. When the gangsters try to take over the theater for a hideout and come upon Kitty and the orphans, Kitty takes one look at Harvey Shapiro, and says, 'Harvey!' And he looks at her and says, 'Kitty!' Then she says, 'Harvey!' again, but this time he looks around to see if his bodyguards are listening and says, 'Call me Legs, baby, call me Legs!' Kitty sighs and they fall in love all over again. Now Kitty asks Legs to help her get back her theater, by going to Mr. Fats and 'persuading' him. Legs knows how to persuade Mr. Fats—pull off his fat and steal it."

Jacques interrupts the tale at this point, and starts picking Mr. Fats' secretaries. "Nowadays we don't call them secretaries, they've got highfalutin titles like 'executive assistants in charge of.' So all of you are going to be called the In-Charge-Ofs. Whenever Mr. Fats wants something done, he calls on the In-Charge-Ofs. Because General Motors —and every company in the whole world—is not run by the president and the chairman of the board, they're run by the In-Charge-Ofs.

"Mr. Fats is a guy who doesn't care that much about the ordinary folk. He's so busy dealing with whole countries that he buys and sells. Hey! That's an idea! Somebody has to be the Amazon, Australia, Africa, we've gotta have people to play the places that Mr. Fats buys and sells. So when Mr.

Fats says something like, 'I want to buy the Amazon' "—
Jacques points to one little girl: "You're going to be the Am-
azon. And your line is, 'No! No! You can't buy me.' Does Mr.
Fats argue with you? No. He sends in the secretary, the In-
Charge-Of."

Like robots, the In-Charge-Ofs move in toward this little
girl, and when they grab her by the throat she turns and looks
at the audience and says, "Yes!" The In-Charge-Ofs have
changed her mind. They drag her off, and everybody dances,
in happiness, worshipping Mr. Fats, and asking, "What'll we
do to make more money, Mr. Fats?"

"Buy Africa."

I cast the whole thing right there in front of the children,
I even make up some of the movements, I get ideas as I talk.
I rarely know what I'm going to do ahead of time. For exam-
ple, I made up the source of Mr. Fats' money right there on
the spot. Pork-belly futures. I'd never heard of pork-belly
futures before I worked on the story of this ballet; now they
keep leaping out of the *Wall Street Journal* at me. Pork-belly
futures are a big thing. Mr. Fats gets into them and runs the
world; so I've named his company Global Growth.

The gangsters get Kitty's theater back by pulling off Mr. Fats' fat. As he gets skinnier, his voice gets higher. In the end there's just skinny little Castellucci in his underwear, saying, "I'm cold."

Next there needs to be some way of letting the audience know that Legs Diamond is being chased by the police. Jacques uses newsboys to tell the story. This is going to be hard, so he picks the best six people, the most energetic, and makes them newsboys. "We're going to dress you all in black and white like newsprint. 'Extra, extra, read all about it! Gangster chief gets out of jail. Legs Diamond loose! D.A. says: 'We'll get that hood.' Hanging judge sets bail. The whole city's after him!"

There's a big chase scene. Diamond tries to make an escape but on come the big cops just as he's escaping. Everyone piles on top of Legs Diamond and he's caught. Is Legs going to jail? Are the cops going to tear him apart? What we need is the mayor to arbitrate. The mayor comes in and says, "Caesar forgave Brutus. Napoleon forgave Josephine. The mayor will forgive you, Legs, if you give back the fat." Everyone goes into a crazy dance telling Legs to give Mr. Fats back his fat. Everybody likes Legs Diamond but they all love Kitty and Legs is helping Kitty. So he can't be all bad!

For the finale to "Fat City," Legs wraps the foam rubber around Mr. Fats until he's all big and fat again. And everybody's happy. Legs is pardoned. Legs and Kitty are together again. Mr. Fats has his fat back and the orphans have their theater. One big happy ending.

He starts piecemeal, and once he stages something he uses hallways and the stage and the costume room and the john—any place he can—to rehearse. And in the end it all fits together.

The Swat Team is special, an elite group—but not elite by virtue of being called elite. You're in the Swat Team because you're faster, smarter, willing to work harder, your imagination is unfettered, you practice on your own, you don't chew gum, fight, and you're proud of each other; otherwise, Swat is just a word.

As the children begin to develop their dances, they perform for one another, and this makes them not afraid of performing. It sharpens the skill of performing. If the performance is not good, Jacques stops them—they've lost their chance to perform. That makes them *be* good. It also makes them analytical. They sit down, and look at the other performers, and begin to judge them.

Jacques developed the Swat Team to encourage the children to become both spectators and performers. As the gangsters make their entrance everybody else watches. And for the first time it begins to look sloppy.

"It's a pain in the ass," he yells, "to teach you steps again which we've been over and over. You're wasting my time. I'm not going to come here anymore. You're supposed to be the best. Jump! Spend your energy! What are you saving it for? Dying?" The kids are cowed, some of them a little sullen. "Get ready, I'm watching for the JDJ—that stands for Jerk Didn't Jump." Jacques motions toward a boy. "Are you the JDJ?" The boy jumps well.

"Why, that's the best jump I've ever seen." His capacity for immediate approval equals his capacity for immediate disparagement. And when the boy tries again, Jacques says, "Wonderful." Then:

"Newsboys: Places." And if they're slow getting up, he'll say, "Sorry, you're too late. You gotta move fast. The orphans get your turn.

"Orphans—come on over! You've got six claps to get in place. Everybody clap, that's the energy we want to see. Clap your hands." Six claps later the orphans are in place. Then the next time he says, "Newsboys! Places," atomic energy happens and six little boys *streak* from wherever they are.

"You're supposed to run as a bunch, no stragglers," he tells the kids. "When that police team joins the Swat Team we've got to work together. I'll tell you why we can't have any stragglers. Maureen, one of the cops, usually comes in late to class. She's an undercover decoy outside of Macy's dressed as a kind of sloppy bag-lady. She walks up and down outside of Macy's with a bag and a purse as if she's just bought something. She waits till someone grabs her purse, and her job is to hold on and argue and fight with that person until the backup team, which is in a car half a block away watching her, comes zooming up and the cops jump out and say, 'Freeze. Police.' Well once because that backup team got caught in traffic she came to class all beat up. So, no straggling allowed. Be on time. Be early! All you little cops have got to be together. Now I'll give you another chance."

"Okay, finale—and if one kid doesn't know the finale at this stage of the game, they're ruining the whole thing for everybody. So let's run through it. You kids over here do the finale." Jacques points to a small group in the corner that includes Andy. "Everybody else sit down." They can't get through the first two or three steps. Everyone becomes glum and quiet. They all look terrified because they can't do the first two or three steps that they'd been doing every single week in their class at school, and for two months on Saturdays in the Swat Team.

"You can't do the finale. Okay. Listen. Everyone is going to do the finale. Next week is Christmas and if you can't do it by the time you get back from Christmas, you're not going to be in the performance. And that's it. If you don't want to, don't show up. But if you want to be in the performance, you have to learn the finale, and I'm not going to teach it to you. The hell with you, I can't teach you any more. Find somebody, maybe a friend, to help you. But I'm through."

After the Christmas break, out of the small group of kids I had chosen to learn the finale or else, only Andy had shown up and was ready to perform. Andy's parents told me that their entire Christmas had revolved around this kid practicing two hours in the morning and two hours at night. Christmas morning under the Christmas tree, unopened presents, and he was doing the finale, he was always doing the finale.

Andy's mother said, "I can't stay in the room while he does it for you." She was so terrified that I wouldn't use him, she couldn't bear to be there. "I'll step out," Andy's mother said. "But I want you to know, if it means anything, that *I*

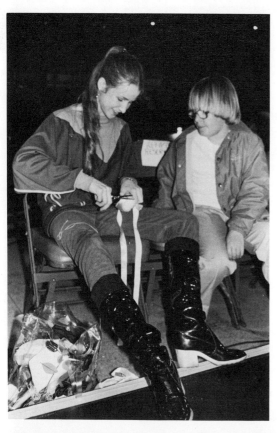

know the finale. . . ." Then she turned away and left. "Okay," I said to the whole class, sure that the kid would be fantastic. "Okay, Andy, I hear you can do the finale, show it to me. Everybody, gather round, Andy's going to do the finale," and all the kids stood around and watched. Andy stood up and started to dance and I could not believe all the mistakes he made. Legs going the wrong way, arms pointing in the wrong direction, but all with such energy and such belief, such strength and honesty, that I didn't know what to do. He was so funny, so serious, and so wrong that I stopped him before he went much further. The whole room fell silent. Nina looked away. I looked straight at Andy and opened my mouth, not knowing what would come out. I'm thinking, Disaster, but what comes out is "Atomic!" "Atomic!" I say. And thirty faces look at me in amazement. They all knew he was a mess. Again I say, "Atomic!" I walk up to him and put my arm around him and his penny eyes shine golden. Then I look around at the class and wink at them and say, "You know, and I know, that there were a few things wrong; right, fellas? A few little things wrong. But they didn't matter. Because I never saw such energy and such, well, atomic energy!" Everything went silent for a long moment and then the whole class burst into applause.

Men and women officers, some dressed in full uniform, swing through the stage door of Lincoln Center past the row of cellophane-wrapped floral bouquets that are ready for the stars of the evening's ballet performance. A huddle of thin young New York City Ballet dancers looking over the week's rehearsal schedule on the bulletin board give the cops cautious smiles. The officers' coats bulge with nightsticks and holsters. Some, undercover agents or narcotics squad police, arrive in casual street clothes, their warm-up suits in the athletic bags slung over their backs.

It is the opening class for the spring season. The cops, about twelve in number, exchange greetings and Jacques meets many of the newcomers with more hugs. When Mary, a plump, smiling black woman, whom Jacques had described earlier as "the victim of a bullet wound caused by a shooting while on duty," walks in, several of the officers give her a warm embrace. During the rehearsal it is evident that her fellow officers maintain a particularly protective and supportive attitude toward her. She moves her lips, mouthing the count as she dances.

The men and women officers, dressed in warm-up suits, take up their positions in the rehearsal room. They lay their guns and nightsticks down over by the piano. Over the next

fifteen minutes more late arrivals trickle in. There is never a word of criticism as they take their places. "How can you criticize them for being late?" Jacques says. "You never know where they're coming from. One guy in the narcotics squad had to sit on a stakeout under the George Washington Bridge for days." Although Jacques explains his teaching police officers to dance by saying their "macho" presence as role models will help overturn the image of dance being a sissyish activity, his emotional connection with the police seems to flow from a boyish admiration for what he sees as their colorful life lived on the edge.

It's Monday night; most people are tired. I'm kinda tired. I usually teach the police class with Nina helping me, and Michael playing the piano. The State Theater is dark; there are no performances on Monday and a studio is always available. The manager of the theater is an ex-cop, and he's delighted to see the police in his theater. The atmosphere for the cops is one of welcome and delight. Sometimes they take a few classes and disappear; either they're on assignment somewhere, or they lose interest. I never know, and I never worry. The minute I come in I put them to work dancing, and we dance without a stop for an hour. Sometimes they come in uniform. They use the upstairs locker room to change in. I remember once being in the locker room when Adam, a black officer, was changing. He had a brown-handled automatic strapped to his ankle and his white cotton

Fruit of the Loom underwear, the kind I wore as a child, contrasted with his beautiful brown skin.

"Adam, how did you get into the police force?" He's very quiet, speaks very softly, but boy, I'd sure like Adam on my side.

"I went into the service out of high school like all the guys did, and when I got out of the marines, I wanted to be a singer in Broadway shows. But I didn't know how to sing. All of my marine buddies said, Let's get into the police force. So I thought I'd give it a try for a few years, while I took singing lessons. But here I am still with the force."

"Well, how long have you been a policeman, Adam?"

"I joined ten years ago."

I said, "You're still doing it; you must be good at it."

And he said, "Well, I guess I'm good. At least they tell me I'm good. They think I'm cool. They think I'm not scared. They all want to be with me because they think I know what to do. I don't know what to do; I'm scared just like the rest of them. And when I'm scared I get silent. I say to myself Quiet, don't say anything before you think, don't do anything before you think, don't do anything till you're sure. My heart's beating fast, but everybody thinks that I'm calm! It's kind of like performing, I guess."

Adam has a little bald spot on the top of his head and he's a *sensational* dancer, so good I think he could go into a Broadway show right now. He has integrity, honesty, works hard.

He worked with another guy named Stan, a white man with a beard; they used to work as a team, mostly busting drug pushers. They both come to class, they dance and forget about the work they do; they're my stars. Adam is a phenomenon. I love him.

There's another big, husky Irish cop with a razor-sharp mind and a wonderful use of language. He grew up in the same neighborhood as Jacques, but he's a few years younger. His name is Sean.

The class always begins with warm-up exercises. Some of the men, whose ages seem to run from twenty-five to their early forties, move rather stiffly.

Two beefy young cops keep being brought up front but seem to keep filtering their way back to the safety of the last row. Trailing them, Jacques' assistant, Nina, goes back to work with the men, who are desperately looking at their feet and then furtively glancing at Jacques to see how they're doing.

"Now," says Jacques, moving to the back of the class,

"turn around—the last row will be the first row." The two cops sigh; there is no escape.

Jacques lunges, his arm shoots forward and he points his finger, then addresses the mirror in an angry voice—"Son of a bitch! Watch out! Son of a bitch, you did it!" The cops, catching some of Jacques' enthusiasm for the comic book cops-and-robbers hyperbole, copy him. His action and words seem extemporaneous. From the outset of class they have been bullied into a rapid series of dance movement with no spoken overview of what it is they're doing. As immediate and warm as Jacques is in welcoming the police, he is also disorienting, pulling them into the vortex of fast percussive movement without explanation, except for occasional image words like "heavy shoe." "Make noise with your feet," Jacques says. "Good. Now lemme show you—make like ya got iron shoes. Take your heavy shoe. . . ." Jacques makes a slow low turn, back straight, emphatically swinging his right leg over his bent left knee. A dignified, slightly pot-bellied lieutenant in the narcotics squad resolutely follows the step.

"C'mon," Jacques pleads, "move." The adults dance

stolidly without the large gestures and ebullience of the children. There are exceptions. One is Rita, a heavily made-up woman with startlingly bright peroxided hair and exaggerated Daisy Mae figure. ("She's in the vice squad," Jacques whispered to Nina before class started. "Sits in the movie houses, waits for old men to grab her knee.") Rita swings through the steps with the calm grace of a t'ai chi expert.

"Now, Sean," Jacques says, "here's what you did on that. It's a stiff-legged walk like a mummy coming out of a crypt. You've got to try for gorgeous arms—eagle-wing arms." He crouches low, with his arms up. "You just did the robot step like the March of the Tin Soldiers. Let's do the rock step, arms flung up, chest in front," he says, looking at Rita, "two of everything in front—landmarks . . ." The class laughs.

Jacques says, "Now I'd like to see all the men run through it."

As the policemen start to go through their routine, Adam moves to the front and starts kidding with Sean. "You just don't have rhythm," Adam says, "like we do. You didn't live in an all-black neighborhood." Sean, concentrating hard, does indeed wind up facing backwards.

Jacques stops the police chorus line, shouting, "YOU! FREEZE! You're facing the wrong way—turn around. I see what works for you," says Jacques, rolling his eyes.

"Police brutality," says Michael, the piano player, not missing a beat.

I teach the cops just like I teach the children. I demand the best. We're all in it together, and one of us is the leader, and I treat the cops that way. I cajole them and we play together using fantasy and exchanging ideas. The curious thing is, except for one or two instances, the children are more dexterous—faster—although the police bring an adult determination and the will to stick with a step much longer. The children are more easily distracted.

I usually start with simple calisthenics and exercises. I get them to begin to distinguish their right leg from their left, exactly the same way I do with children. I divide them up, make roles for them, keep them constantly moving. At the end of class I give them a warm-down; and we usually do one movement with everybody dancing together. I try and keep all the movements fairly simple; it's important to try and make them not look down. Most people who are trying to make their feet move in a certain way look at their feet. Then, if they've finally got it, and you make them look up, they can't do the step anymore, because somehow or other they're not watching their feet. Right from the beginning I try and get them to use the mirror, because eventually the mirror will become the audience. And dancers have to move with their heads up.

I don't tell them about the performance initially. I tell them that we're going to work on a dance together; if it's good and they would like to they can get a chance to perform it; if not, we won't do it, whatever they decide. And they all seem to accept that and not be afraid of it. They're very suspicious about being used or manipulated. The cops make a real effort to come here; and that decision places them a cut above the ordinary person.

Scarlett and Lisa are friends. Lisa's a little bit taller than Scarlett. They're both very bright girls, beautiful girls. Lisa wears Gucci outfits, she's blond, takes dancing lessons and is extremely bright yet very shy. Scarlett is not as pretty as Lisa but far more aggressive—definitely the leader.

When the orphans came together for the first time, I grabbed the girl nearest me and said, "All right. You're going to be the orphan that Kitty, the Wonder-Woman mother, likes best. You're going to be right in center, and your signature is that your thumb's in your mouth all the time." By sheer chance, that girl was Lisa. She cuddles up close to Kitty right in the center of the orphans, and she leads the pack. They all do the same dance, more or less, but Lisa is in the center.

Once, in a rehearsal, I said, "All the orphans together," and Scarlett ran up to me saying, "Lisa's late, Lisa's not here. I can do it, though, I know it! Let me do it." And immediately

her thumb went in her mouth and she started doing Lisa's role perfectly.

I said, "Listen, Scarlett. You're bugging me. You're climbing on top of me all the time. Don't worry about Lisa, just worry about yourself. I'll decide if Lisa is going to be replaced or not and who is going to do it."

And the amazing thing is, I guess you could say I'd been rough on her, but it didn't faze her. She got a disappointed look for a moment, but she bounded right back, never losing her place, right up in front of the class. If I put Lisa and Scarlett in the back of the room, with twenty children or thirty in front of them, by the time the exercise is over Lisa's in the middle of the pack and Scarlett's up front. If I turn to the right, I trip over Scarlett. If I turn to the left, if I step back, I bump into her. If I say, "Everybody move back" she shuffles a few inches in place. It's amazing. The reason is, of course, Scarlett's enormous intelligence and a desire not to let a thing go by, to see and experience everything.

When these two girls are not dancing the two of them stand together. Scarlett is always talking; she always has a comment to make to Lisa, but never looks at her. She doesn't want to miss anything, her eyes are wandering all over the room; she watches and makes comments about everything.

There's one day toward the end of the year when it's time to try to bring all the elements together—Swat, the police class, the stars who are going to perform with the kids, the music and the narration. Up to this point everybody has been learning separately and there's a real need to bring it all together. They all know the plot but they don't understand why they have to run to the right and duck on a certain note, while the orphans run to the left and do something else. Now they'll discover that when they separate the police are going to dance down the middle. All this separate choreography somewhere or other has to be put together, and this is the day.

I have to stage everything—the entrances and the exits, the total look of the piece—in this one class and it's the first time I've got them together so I go like a maniac of energy. I'm all over the room; I demand everyone to be in place listening to me, and able to react immediately. As the number starts I'm yelling all kinds of things: "Gangsters come on

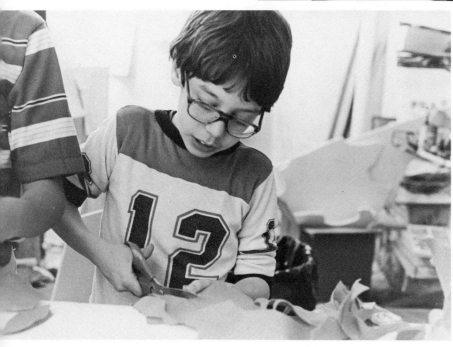

from the left! You should be right in the middle of them! Brandon, you're too far to the side! Orphans, stage right, be ready! The music's too fast! Are you watching? This is where you should have your dark glasses, Carol." I'm the only one who knows everything, and I'm trying now to explain to everyone at the same time what they're seeing and how their part fits in. At first, I think I may confuse them. But when they see it come together they begin to understand. The orphans understand *why* they run to the left and duck: it's because someone's gonna jump over 'em, and it's Chris in his role as Legs Diamond. It's the first day he's come to really rehearse. He may have been around before, but he's always been saving himself. Today he jumps over them.

Martin Charnin has written lyrics to "Fat City." Janet Eilber is to be the Wonder Woman. Christopher d'Amboise is to be the gangster. Jacques has met separately with the professionals and choreographed their part of the dance. The newsboys have already had a costume fitting with Susan Crile and Carol Wentz, the designers. Now it's that special Saturday morning when the police join the Swat Team to rehearse "Fat City."

Everyone's in place but then something happens. Nina rushes over and says, "I've got to talk to you, Jacques. You forgot someone."

"What do you mean?"

"I didn't say anything all this time because I thought you had a special reason. But you forgot Andy. He's not a gangster. He's not an orphan. He's not a cop. He's not a newsboy. But he wants to do a dance. He wants a part."

I had completely forgotten about him after his finale disaster. "What am I going to do with Andy? I don't know. What shall I do about Andy?" I look around for him, I can't even find him. He's been hiding in the corner, without a part, thinking that I don't want to use him. I'd just forgotten about him—he's been in the back all this time trying to learn everything so he'd be ready when I gave him a part. I spot him at last in a corner. He looks up at me and I look at him, thinking, It's terrible that I've forgotten to give him a role. "What am I going to do with Atomic Andy?" I exclaim. "Why, he's the most crucial guy in the show! I've been saving him for the end! Attention, everybody! The newsboys are telling you the news, but where do they get it? From the newspapers. Andy supplies the newspapers. The whole city runs on what you read in the papers. So Andy, you're going to come in with this big bag full of newspapers, you're going to hand them to the newsboys and that's where they're going to find out that Legs Diamond is a wanted man. There are going to be a lot

of difficult dance steps—it's a hard part but you can do it.'' The class looks at Andy thinking what a fantastically lucky guy he is.

I always try to get at least one or two well-known people in the arts and costume design to come and work with the children. They have to costume from odds and ends. We can't buy costumes or make them, it's too expensive. Sneakers have to be made to look like boots. Blue jeans have to be made to look like buckskin. Some little device has to be used to establish a whole character.

Carol Wentz created many of the costumes for "Fat City.'' She made a hat full of bananas and fruit for the little girl who plays the Amazon. The Amazon is dressed in her school outfit and sneakers—but she's wearing this banana-fruit hat when Mr. Fats yells out, "Buy the Amazon.'' The dark glasses and the white ties and red carnations for the gangsters make them gangsters; they don't need anything else. The little police wear blue T-shirts and blue pants and

have a gold paper badge safety-pinned on their shirts. The real policemen wear their uniforms. The artist Barbara Bellin designed the costumes for the orphans, who are dressed as if they found their clothes in the basement of the theater where they'd been living—snatches of old costumes and rags and chiffon things. Some wear discarded toe shoes; one is barefoot; one orphan has one high-heel shoe and one sneaker; one has pearls around her neck; one has a boa; another is in an old discarded tutu—a hodgepodge of odds and ends.

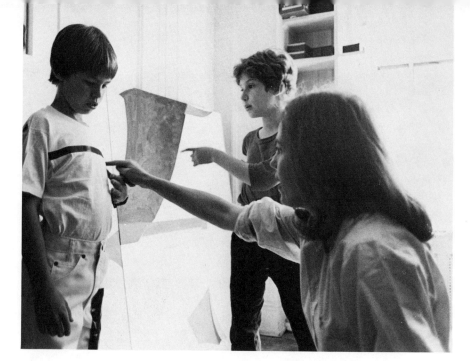

Susan Crile took six or seven of the little newsboys to her studio. First she fitted their costumes and then she asked them to stand side by side against the wall so that she could look at them, change around the different black and white patterns her newsboy costumes made. It was especially good that she was at the Saturday rehearsals because she could see how well the choreography worked with the design as the kids shuttle in and out, do-si-do, and the black and white patterns change. It turned out to be very effective.

The cops are the biggest stars, bigger than Mary Tyler Moore, bigger than Judy Collins, who will host the show. And yet the kids react very strangely to them; they stare and they get very still as they watch the police dance.

Sam Edwards, the deaf interpreter and signer, was standing with all the deaf boys watching the police dance for the first time, and he started to laugh. I asked, "What's so funny?" and Sam said, "The boys are signing: 'Gee, the cops don't dance so hot.'"

"Tell them that they get better as they go along. And not to be so hard on them."

Brian Drummond has been dancing since September, and is extraordinary, the best in his school, one of the best dancers in the Swat Team; he's conscientious, bright. Every time I say, "Is there a volunteer?" Brian volunteers. If he doesn't volunteer the kids turn around and point to him and say, "Brian can do it." I overheard Brian go over to Adam, the black cop who's a fabulous dancer, and ask him, "Are you really a cop?"

And Adam says, "Yeah. Only it's called a policeman."

"Where's your gun?"

Adam smiles and says, "I'm an undercover policeman. I'm undercover. So you can't find it, it's hidden."

Then Brian, changing the subject, looks at him and says, "You know, you're a pretty good dancer. In fact, I think you're the best of them."

The children, deaf children included, like to watch one another perform. But after they've seen a performance once, unless someone is spectacular, they ignore it. They have no need to see it repeated. Except for the police. Whenever the police dance, all the children stop to watch, and they eagerly watch them perform over and over again.

The first dress run-through.

"It's a mess," Jacques says. "A week ago it was a helluva lot better. 'Fat City' should be a show-stopper. None of you know what you're doing. Even my own son doesn't know what he's doing. Can you tell us the words for the gangster song? Let's at least get that right."

"A man of mild persuasion . . . We'll control the situation . . ." Michael accompanies Chris on the piano as he sings the new lyrics in uncertain voice.

"Do you know how to go all the way down on the knee slide, Chris?" His father goes down on his knees demonstrating bravely, a wince of pain crossing his face. Leaving the piano, Chris copies him.

"Now," Jacques says to his son, "just walk deadpan toward the audience. Walk slowly up. Look 'em straight in the eye. Slouch—dirty look. Right. Left." Chris follows him. An incongruous father-and-son team—Chris, wan and delicate, reserved, like his mother; Jacques, animated and craggy, outgoing. Nonetheless there is an unusual bond of love and pride between them that parallels Jacques' enormous pride and ambition for some of the more talented children in the Swat Team.

All the children at one time or another have seen the bulletin board in the corner of the practice room covered with ballet graffiti, on which is scribbled "Chris has the name, but will he have the fame?"

Now the police start their dance. They're self-conscious. Up to now they've been in a studio with me and maybe a few visitors watching, or their friends. Now, there's eighty, ninety, a hundred people in this room. There's an audience. There's Judy Collins, Kyra Nichols, Kevin Kline, and me, yelling orders in all directions. The bustle creates a crazy heightened energy that begins to grow here and will continue to grow over the next ten days until the final dress rehearsal just prior to performance. It's wonderful, the very healthy energy of creative, supercharged people ready to go.

I always demand the most, and set the standard as high as possible, which is perfection. I say to my students, "I want this to be perfect." I want them to dance like the best dancers that have ever danced. I want them to behave perfectly, with good manners and taste and concern for each other. I want them to be honest and straightforward and true. I demand all these things on the highest level and I keep demanding it, because I know that the children can stretch themselves and by demanding the best they will stretch themselves to meet it. Some will meet it, and some may not, but the way I'll judge them is by whether or not they've *tried* to meet it. If they try and fail, but try very hard, they're already successful. The attempt is the success. The effort to achieve perfection is the heart and soul of the pro; and to try for less than perfection because it may not be attainable is to fail. So I always demand the most of them.

A professional dancer should make the audience feel that his dancing is an explosion of beauty erupting on the stage. If the dancer is exhausted, or has indigestion, or is bored from doing the same thing every night, he must overcome his problems with skill and discipline. It's the dancer's job to make the audience feel—his focus is no longer on himself but on the audience. I'm often asked, How do you make that feeling happen? I have only one answer: I use everything under the sun.

New York's Felt Forum is a part of Madison Square Garden. It's a gigantic scallop shell. One side is a curtain that runs the length of the wall, maybe two hundred feet. In front of that bluish-gray curtain is the New York Knicks' basketball court, which has been covered in black, non-skid linoleum so the dancers can dance and the floor won't be ruined. On the black linoleum are all kinds of grids and painted shapes. These are strips of tape that have been put into a kind of hop-scotch pattern so that in the finale, when nine hundred or a thousand children take their places on stage, they'll know where to go. St. Patrick's goes to the square of tape with a red marker, and it is a big square because the St. Patrick's

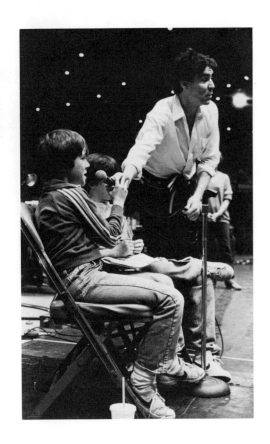

class has one hundred eighty kids. Next to it is a little strip of tape for the Home School, and fifteen kids squeeze into that little square because there are only fifteen kids in the dance program from that school. And so on and so on across the whole stage. The orchestra is set up on the floor in the middle of the front edge of the basketball court and there are big banks of speakers on either side; the overhead grid is covered with hundreds of lights.

The orchestra's in rehearsal, consummate professionals all: eleven musicians and four singers with lots of mikes all over the place. The orchestra will serve as the command center. The seats directly behind the orchestra are not sold because the orchestra blocks the view, there being no orchestra pit. The orchestra is made up of synthesizers and pianos and drums and several other instruments. Throughout the day the orchestra rehearses, not necessarily mindful of anything that's going on on stage. The children may be rehearsing a dance to take place in the middle of the program while the orchestra's playing the finale or the overture. Jacques runs around frantically, using a microphone on a long wire, but by the end of the day his voice is gone anyway.

The children start arriving, usually with a couple of parents, a principal or a teacher in charge. Arrangements are made through the production staff and the school to coordi-

nate how they arrive. The sections way over to the left and right of the orchestra have been ribboned off so that the children will know where to sit. When they're not needed to rehearse they wait in those seats. During the performance they're going to be in the same place. Jacques rehearses with the children how they get on and off stage, using this cordoned-off section as a device to keep them in place. The first school will arrive at noon. They will have about fifteen minutes to rehearse their dance. As they're rehearsing, another school is filing in and finding their places. When the first group, the 12:00-to-12:15 group, is finished, they sit down and the 12:15-to-12:30 group rehearses. Meanwhile, another school comes in and then another. As the day progresses, waves and waves of children arrive, but the waves don't recede. The house fills.

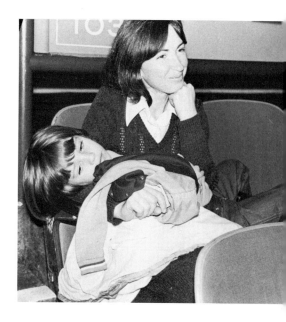

I'm about ready to rehearse "Fat City" when I find out that Andy has broken his arm. Atomic Andy comes over to me terrified and in tears; his arm is in a cast. Andy's mother has been telling him, "Go tell Mr. d'Amboise you've broken your arm and can't dance." But Andy has spent all day in Madison Square Garden and hasn't told me. Finally his mother grabs him, brings him over and with a trembling voice says, "Andy has broken his arm."

All this seems to be happening when I'm at my busiest. I turn around and say, "No. How? My God, how awful! What happened?" And as he's trying to tell me, I'm thinking, He can't dance. I'm half-relieved. That's one less to worry about. At the same time I know how much it means to him. So I say, "Oh, what a shame, what a shame. I'm sorry. Well, I guess you can't dance."

"No, I can do it," he says.

"Andy, you're just going to fall and make it worse."

"I can do it, I can do it."

"That's up to your parents." And the parents look at me and they really feel that he can do it, too. They thought that I might refuse to let him dance because he had a broken arm. "Okay. I won't take responsibility. But if you're careful and everything else works, you can do it."

Then I turn my attention to something else and forget about Andy but a half hour later Andy comes over in tears. He can't dance because he can't get into his black and white newsboy costume. His broken arm won't bend, so he can't fit into the sleeve. Poor Andy is crushed. I have to think fast. I cut off the sleeve and use black tape to make it look like part of the costume. He looks the same as the rest of the newsboys except that this kid has a fat white sleeve with a funny black design on it, and the other kids have thin white sleeves with funny black designs. At the last minute Andy was saved by a

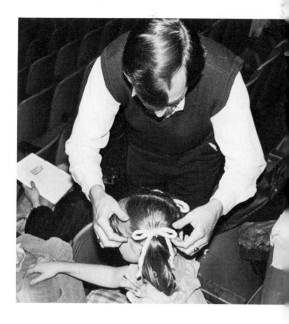

pair of scissors, a little black tape, and a lot of belief and courage to go out and dance. The possibility that he might not be able to dance was a traumatic thing for him. But as it turned out he was able to enjoy the experience and he was wonderful.

Finally a thousand children are in place, ready for the finale. At this point if all goes well it's around 5:00 and there's an hour of rehearsal time left.

I get on the mike, and call out to schools in turn. "Herrick School, could you please come on stage." When Herrick rushes to the stage I show them the square that has been taped down on the floor indicating the Herrick School, then I tell them to sit down and wait. I call another school, and they come in and sit down. This is the first time they discover their places for the finale. I have been rehearsing them throughout the year to come on from the right and leave from the right, or to come on from the left wing and leave from the left. But it takes almost an hour to get all those children on the stage just in the right place. Then they run through the finale. Now it's 6:00. We have to get off the stage for a dinner break; otherwise there's an enormous overtime problem with the stagehands, who have already bent the rules every way they could for us. I tell the children, "Quietly now, you've got an hour and a half for dinner, then you've got to return to your seats, ready to go. Don't forget to pick up any junk that you've left."

The heroic teachers and principals and mothers handle

these thousand kids in the very crazy neighborhood that surrounds Madison Square Garden. They get 'em fed, they get 'em back, and somehow they don't lose any. In that hour and a half, I'm all over the place. I have some assistants to help me with last-minute instructions: "Remember to tell Herrick that they were on too early," or "Lee, the tempo for Herrick was too slow."

Lee Norris, the conductor, is almost as tense as I am, and we always have a fight. We go off together, angry scowls on our faces, to some out-of-the-way corner of the theater or the dressing room and have it out. Eventually we come back with smiles and everything goes on. It's been a tradition, it happens every year. Except this year, no fight. In the dressing room right before the show Lee turns around and says to me, "We didn't have a fight." I say, "What do we do?" He says, "We gotta stage one. It'll be bad luck if we don't have a fight." So we go out to the center of the floor and yell at each other for a few minutes so that the tradition can keep going.

Lee Norris is a unique man. I could not do the performance without Lee. As a musician, as a personality, as a character, as an energetic force, he's a phenomenal man. He's full of love and concern for people and children in particular. We work very, very alike. God sent him for us to work together. He calls me at four o'clock in the morning and says, "I'm about to take a flight, I'm here in California, and I'm flying back on the red eye, so I'll have some time to work on the score. Listen to this! I've written this!" and he starts to sing to me over the phone his latest idea. He's wonderful, wonderful. He's one of the pillars that hold up the National Dance Institute.

A lot of the children have never seen a conductor before. They don't even know what a conductor is. I used to cue the kids with, "All ready now, five, six, seven, eight, go!" And halfway through one year I realized, I'm not going to be there when they perform, to say Five, six, seven, eight, go! They're going to have to learn how to watch the conductor. Now I tell the kids just that—"I'm not going to be around to say five, six, seven—you're going to have to learn to watch the conductor." After six months of hearing You've gotta watch the conductor, one little kid got the courage to come over and say, "What conductor?" They thought I meant the bus conductor! Or the subway conductor. It was the first time I realized a lot of those kids had never seen an orchestra. So now what I do is put one person right up front to be the leader, and I make sure that the kid understands exactly how to

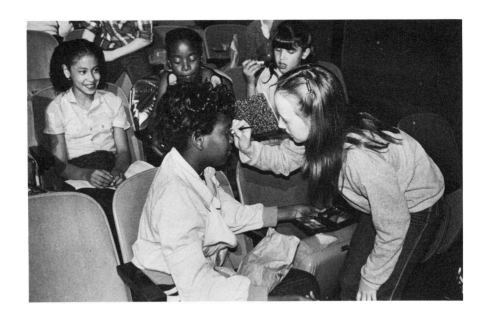

watch the conductor to get the beat. I tell the others, "Okay, watch the conductor but if it's too dark or there's a light in your eyes, watch Brian Drummond up front. When he starts, you start." I usually use my best person; the one who's the sharpest, the most with it. I know I'm safe with Brian leading that finale. It doesn't matter what kind of beat Lee Norris is going to do, Brian is gonna get it and be on it. He's my security.

Half-hour till the show starts. The audience is coming in. There are friends in the audience, parents; it's the most wonderful atmosphere, everybody knows they're in for a good time. The orchestra is tuning up. Children are running all over the place in excitement, waving at each other and their parents as they come in. But mostly something fascinating is happening. In a curious way, the children are now professionals. If they're nervous, or fearful, it's kept under control. Everyone seems very busy preparing for the performance. Making sure their costumes are right. Going over the sets. Helping each other. Practicing their entrances and exits.

It's exactly the atmosphere that I remember when I was a professional dancer. Now, watching all the excitement around me, I want to do this—be a part of all this; but I'm not the performer anymore. There's not anything that I can focus on to do, my function is over. It's the performers' show now; the director and choreographer must become spectators. If I go over to talk to any of the performers, they don't want to talk to me. They're busy preparing for the show. I don't belong anymore on their side of the footlights. I belong in the audience.

Everyone seems to have grown in stature. A kind of control and authority has come over all the children. Two hours before when we broke, they were all nervous, frightened children who didn't know what they were going to do. There wasn't enough rehearsal time, they wished they had more rehearsal time. "What do we do, what do we do?" they all asked. But now it's a half-hour to showtime and the audience is coming in; they're tuning up, and they're a thousand professionals. My heart is beating faster. Do my friends have an unobstructed view? Is that parent sitting on the side where their son or daughter will be performing? I start hanging around with the stars. Is there anything I can do? They're just like the kids. They smile, and they say, Yeah, let me go over my script, I'll talk to you later, I'm busy, I'm preparing. I feel like there's nothing for me to do. So I sit down up front, and start to sweat nervously. Then the performance starts. And all the things come together. Everything fits and melds, all the children that I was worried about make their entrances and exits. I turn to look, hoping they'll remember they come on here. I look for them and I see they're in place. I'm worried that the lights aren't going to come on bright enough at this spot, and just as I worry about it, they come on bright enough. It's all like clockwork.

Then somewhere within the course of the first half-hour, I stop worrying, and I cross the bridge into being a spectator, and I sit and I start to laugh with delight and applaud; I start enjoying the show. The children are going in and out from the audience to the stage, making their entrances and returning; they've been watching their classmates and other schools perform, as spectators, knowing that in ten minutes the roles will be reversed. Back and forth they go, on and off stage throughout the two hours; a shuffle from spectators to performers back to spectators, to such a degree that the adult audience now feels as though they're performing. It's what every piece of theater attempts to do, to make the audience and the performers one, in celebration of whatever the play's about, and we achieve it in celebration of the joy of dance.

A special kind of hush comes over the audience. "Fat City" is about to be performed. In the running order of the show, "Fat City" is the last thing before the finale. It is the Swat Team's number, it has the police in it, it has the stars, it is the featured act. " 'Fat City,' take your places for 'Fat City.' "

Right before the performance I was trying to get to the bathroom for the first time that day when Scarlett came rushing over, oozing words and tears and excitement and said, "Lisa is sick—Lisa hasn't come, Lisa is not here, and there's no one to be the thumb-sucking orphan."

I turned on my heel to her and said angrily, "Boy, so you've finally got what you wanted. I bet you're happy. So you're gonna do it. You're gonna do that role."

And she looked at me stunned, and said, "Oh, no, I could never do it, Lisa's my best friend. Somebody else has to do it. I want to keep her as my friend. I can't hurt her. It would hurt her too much."

I was stunned. It was fantastic. Fantastic. It turned out that Lisa came anyway. She's an old pro. She came in just in time to do "Fat City." I had misjudged Scarlett, and misjudged their friendship. But I was very pleased. There was an *esprit de corps.*

The kids also knew that after "Fat City" the big finale comes—the climax of the show. It would be the last time they'd dance. The Swat Team were all larger than life. They'd grown a little taller in their minds, they were stronger, more elegant, more fantastic. Except little Andy, who was in a big trauma in the wings. Because of his broken arm, he couldn't carry his bag of newspapers. He was swinging the bag all around, trying to solve his problem; the more he tried the more it wrapped around his neck. He was getting choked by the bag—a real newsboy's bag from the *Newark Star Ledger.* The poor little guy was in tears again and he didn't know what to do. Nina switched the bag over to his other side; it was nothing, it just meant that he had to wear it over the other shoulder, but he wanted to be perfect, and I had said, "You carry it over your left shoulder." Switching to the right shoulder, he thought, was all wrong. Nina just calmly gave him a kiss, switched it and said, "Don't worry, Jacques won't mind. In fact, it'll look even better on the right side."

"Fat City" itself went along without a hitch. The police were standing in the wings counting "A hundred three, a hundred four, a hundred five, a hundred six: Go!"—counting their entrances so they wouldn't miss them, all of them counting on Adam to lead them. The orphans with Kitty were absolutely secure, looking great in their costumes; the newsboys, wonderful in their black and white costumes. The real cops and the little cops all eager; the Amazon, the bottom half of Africa, all in place; Mr. Fats wrapped up in his fat being carried around by dancers from the Alvin Ailey company, four strapping strong talented young men. The police get their man, Legs Diamond gets his girl, Mr. Fats gets back his fat—"Fat City" is a huge success.

When it was over I thought that you could have taken "Fat City" and put it in any Broadway show and it would have worked. It had everything in it, the songs, music, personality, imagination, lyrics, the zaniness of it all—it was what I had hoped to do.

The Felt Forum performance is called the Event of the Year because it takes a whole school year to produce. We begin with no idea of what's going to happen at the end of the year, but the momentum builds. Schools keep joining, more kids keep coming in, finally the program begins to have a form, a finale is done, music is written, plots are devised, solos are assigned, the children work on perfecting their parts, costumes are made; stars begin to join, the media begin to pay attention; a theater is booked; tickets are sold. There are final rehearsals; a local performance in each of the schools is done as a preview, giving the kids a chance to perform in front of their classmates, and then it all comes together: once in Madison Square Garden. Just once. And after it's over, it's never performed again. The kids go on to the next grade; they're not a part of the program anymore. There is a new group of children to audition, and the entire process starts all over again.

We have no idea, as one year ends, what the next year is going to bring, what kind of children we're going to get, what's going to happen. The event itself has a special significance for everyone concerned because they've all been intimately involved in its evolution. And after it's over, you can't recreate it.

On Teaching
and the Magic of Dance

There seems to be a human need to dance—to dance for joy, for sadness, to petition the gods and then to thank them. Children feel this need to dance acutely; often it's just the opportunity, the invitation, they lack. It is, I'm sure, this human need that triggers the extraordinary changes I see in them. At the National Dance Institute we expose a thousand children a year to the mystery of dance—some who are deaf, some who don't know left from right, and some who never thought they could (or would even want to) dance—and all of them are changed by the experience, some in small ways, others profoundly.

In order to be free, in order to create, in order to learn, a student has to have limits imposed by his teacher. Students have to be given a framework within which to create. If you tell a class to "make up anything you like," what you get is chaos. But impose a limit, "Make up anything you like, but do it in one foot square," and you have the beginnings of creative thinking. Add another limit: "Now still in one foot square, invent some movements that last thirty seconds (not twenty-five or thirty-two, it has to be thirty), and you've introduced the concept of time. Next I might say to the class, "One thing you did, one gesture, was more interesting than another. Do you want to use it at the beginning of the exercise or at the end?"

That choice, that limitation, speaks to a very complex notion—the dramatic implications of gesture. Then I might say, "What kind of music do you want to put to this dance that takes place in one foot square, in thirty seconds exactly, with gestures that build dramatically?" And the choice the child makes of a Scott Joplin rag instead of a march will have an effect on all the decisions he has already made up to this point. This exercise, this imposition of limits, defines choreography. Choreography is the communication of an idea, using ordered and structured gesture, in time (a thirty-second rag) and space (one foot square). A far cry from chaos.

The teacher/choreographer becomes the human link in the transmission of the mystery that is dance. The children learn *through* me. They learn because I am the latest part of a continuous chain. They learn because I was carefully taught. And now it is my responsibility to teach them with care.

Jacques d'Amboise